MY MERRY MENAGERIE

My Merry Menagerie

Lighthearted Verses & Drawings

Rosemary Butler

Sun on Earth™ Books
Heathsville, Virginia

Published by Sun on Earth™ Books

www.sunonearth.com

Illustrations by the author.

Publisher's Cataloging-in-Publication Data
Butler, Rosemary.
    My merry menagerie / Rosemary Butler.— Ist ed.
      p. cm.
    ISBN: 978-1-883378-22-6
          1. Animals—Poetry.
          I. Title.

PS3613.U8 M9 2013
811'.6—dc23

Library of Congress Control Number: 2013944217

ISBN: 978-1-883378-22-6

These lighthearted verses
Are best read aloud,
Out in the sunshine
Or under a cloud.

I wrote them especially
To brighten your day.
Perhaps they may not,
But I do hope they may!

— ROSEMARY BUTLER

INTRODUCTION

The first time I wrote a light verse for an audience was when my husband and I were living on the island of Luzon in the Philippines. The occasion was a hillside party to watch the sun go down behind a mountain. The setting for the party was a lonely hillside clearing, which our hostess had elegantly transformed with oriental rugs, linen tablecloths, and silver champagne buckets. In keeping with the spirit of the affair, I wore a white strapless dress, a challenging choice for the remote and grassy site. This singular soirée turned out to be a smashing success!

The guests had been asked to come to the party with some form of entertainment to amuse the other guests. One played a guitar, another sang, others told stories and jokes. For my contribution to the party, I had written a light verse about watching the sun setting behind a mountain, the very theme of the affair. My recitation was well received with a hearty round of applause.

Years later, we and the rest of the world learned that the mountain we had watched that evening was Mt. Pinatubo, the volcano which erupted so violently that the countryside for twenty miles around, including our party site, was covered with several feet of ash!

I have written light verse for many years, then tucked it away for another day. As a child, I always liked hearing light verse read aloud to me. The bouncy rhythms, clever rhymes, and sometimes silly words appealed to my sense of fun. I loved Ogden Nash's verses, especially the ones he wrote for Camille Saint-Saëns's "The Carnival of the Animals." They were my inspiration for the verses in this book.

My Merry Menagerie consists of animals, bugs, and crawly creatures. I have written these verses for precocious preadolescents and lighthearted adults. My hope, dear reader, is that you are one of these.

Rosemary Butler, 2013

THE ALLIGATOR

A woman, who is much too fat,

Has photographed her pussycat.

Then snapped one of an alligator,

Who smiled at her, and promptly ate her.

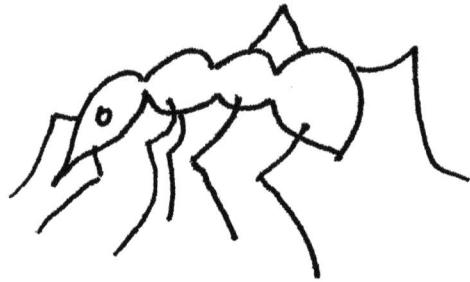

ANTS

"Here," said the ant,

"Is my family tree:

My Ant Father, Ant Mother,

And, of course, there is me.

There are millions of others.

To name them, I can't,

Except for Ant Uncle,

And dear old Ant Aunt."

THE ARMADILLO

"I must have a four-poster bed,"

Said the arrogant old armadillo.

"A smooth satin sheet

For my toes and my feet,

Plus a heavenly blue goose-down pillow."

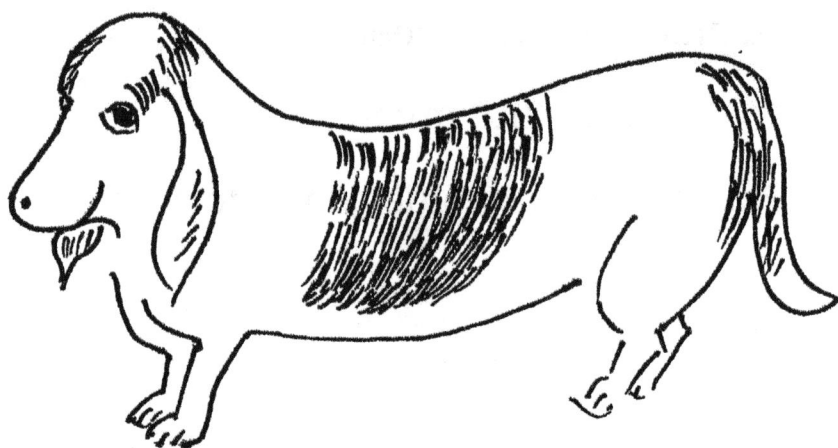

THE BASSET HOUND

The sassy, classy basset hound

Originally came from France.

His legs are short, his ears are long,

And his mind is on romance.

A BAT

When you meet a female bat,

Please don't tell her that she's fat.

CAMELS

Camels live where it is hot
And often dream that they were not
Confined to dull and arid spaces,
But long for cool and English places.
To be under the trees
In the Forest of Arden,
Or stroll through the flowers
In Anne Hathaway's garden.
And leave all the walking
Through deserty wastes
To beasts which possess
Less fanciful tastes.
I wonder if camels
Have ever thought
That their heavenly home
Was Camelot?

A CAT

A cat is apt to catch a cold

When he is sick or when he's old.

So hand him a warm and woolly blankey

And a properly monogrammed linen hankie.

CHAMELEONS

Chameleons like to change

The color of their skin

From the color it is now,

To the color it has been.

Chameleons run along the walls,

And sometimes one chameleon falls.

They cling to walls on suction cups.

I'd say they have their downs and ups.

A COW

How

Should a cow,

Sweet or mean,

Meet the Queen?

Simply bow.

THE DIK-DIK

The dik-dik is an antelope

From Africa, of course.

He runs so fast he thinks he is

A famous racing horse.

To time his running speed

He often wears a clock.

Tick, tock, tock, tick.

There goes the fast dik-dik.

DRAGONS

The dragon, earth's most fabulous beast,
Is found in cultures West and East.

The western ones have homely hides,
Wet scaly feet, iron-clad insides.
The whole effect is rather raunchy,
Since western dragons are old and paunchy.

The eastern ones are more refined
From jade-smooth head to sleek behind.
They look at home on red silk pillows
Reclining under weeping willows.

Both kinds have faces fierce or pouting,

And nostrils forever spouting

Incensed flames, the oriental ones;

Fire and brimstone, the occidental ones.

You'll really get a fiery jag on

By being with either kind of dragon.

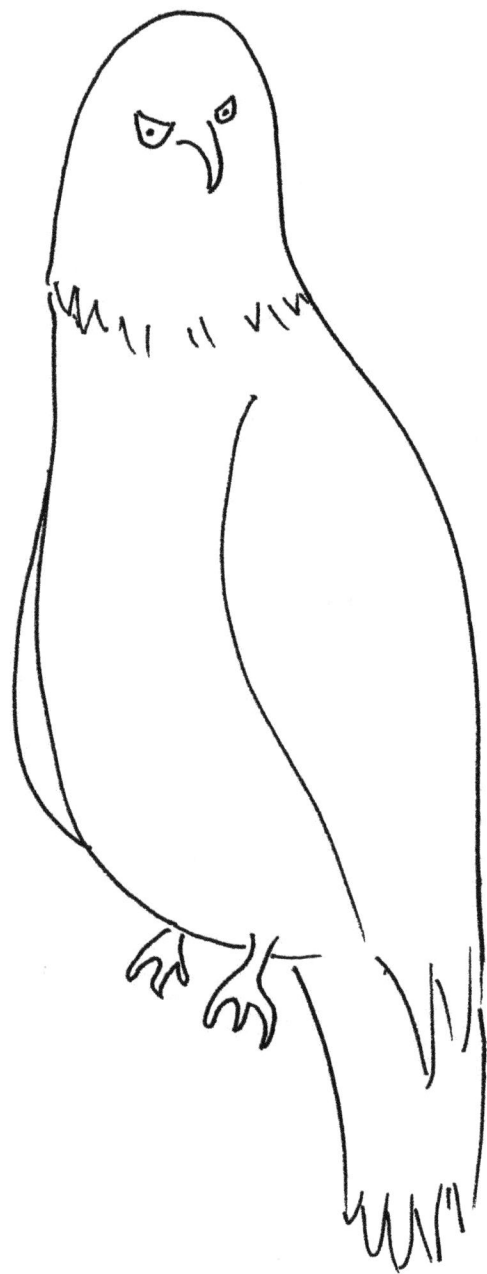

EAGLES

Eagles have feathers

From head to toe.

That's just the way

Their feathers grow.

Then why are

American eagles

Called:

Bald?

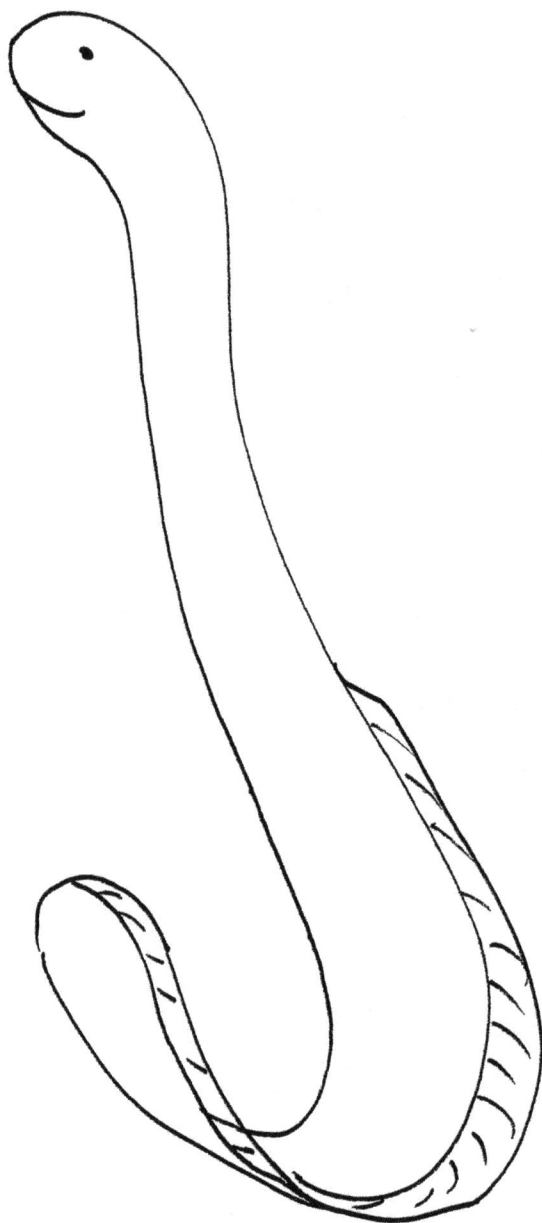

AN EEL

I've been to Belgium
And eaten an eel.
It was quite a meal,
A marvelous meal,
But I hoped that the chef
Hadn't made a mistake
And served snake.

All of the while
I was eating that dish,
That delectable dish,
That savory dish,
I kept telling myself
Again and again
"Think FISH".

THE EGRET

Here is a pet

You should never forget.

So invite your egret

To a pink champagne fête.

FAWNS

Fawns wander through the piney woods

At dusk and also dawn.

Debussy wrote of another time

In his "Afternoon of a Faun."

THE FOX

The fox who will not take a bath

Has committed a terrible gaffe.

Call him somewhat obnoxious:

A pox on his foxness.

With friends he'll elicit a laugh.

ANOTHER FOX

A frugal old financier fox

Hides his money away in a box.

Also well-chosen stocks

Are kept safe under locks

In his personal private Ft. Knox.

THE FROG

Observe the frog upon the stump:

Complexion rather bumpy,

Body green and fairly plump,

Disposition grumpy.

But though he seems a frumpy lump,

The dumpy frog can really jump!

A GNU

I once knew a gnu

Who asked, "Do you know

What is new with us gnus?"

I hadn't a clue.

So I had to refuse

To answer the gnu,

Who replied,

"Well, no gnus

Is good news!"

THE GOAT

The goat has quite an appetite,

And if you care to let him,

He loves to party through the night.

No cuisine has ever upset him;

To leave is difficult to get him.

And when there breaks dawn's early light,

He's eaten everything in sight.

THE HAMSTER

The hamster is always a ham.

He hams it up when he can.

He's a serious fan

Of George Hamilton,

And especially likes Hamilton's tan.

HEDGEHOGS

Hedgehogs toddle through the woods

In coats of spiny bristles,

Looking like pillows stuck with pins

Or ambulating thistles.

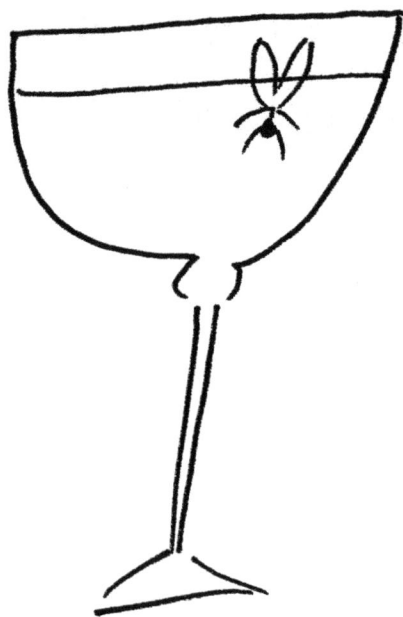

THE HOUSE FLY

The house fly always flies

In search of a tiny pool,

Especially one of cocktail size,

To plunge in vodkas, rums, and ryes.

Swimming around and around he tries

To find where buried treasure lies,

Until he finally sinks and dies —

A grave both 80 proof and cool.

THE IBEX

The ibex is a mountain goat,

A ruminating animal,

Who likes to leap from peak to peak:

A fleet four-footed Hannibal.

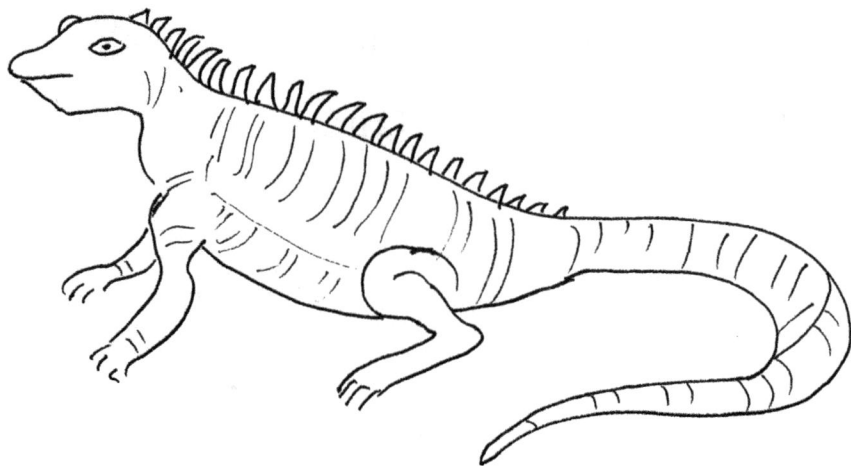

AN IGUANA

The parents of four-year-old Lancelot

Asked him, "What kind of pet do you want?

A dog or a cat? Or something like that?

No, of course, what you want is a horse!"

"NO," said their son,

"I wanna IGUANA!"

THE JAGUAR

The most famous English cat by far

Is cat, of course,

And also car.

A KODIAK BEAR

If you dislike your neighbors

Just give them a scare,

And tell them your pet

Is a Kodiak bear!

THE LION

The lion never tells a lie.

He always tells the truth.

He likes to be like Lincoln,

And not like John Wilkes Booth.

THE LYNX

The lynx wears a brown brocaded coat,

Laced loosely underneath him,

Tufted ears and furry ruff:

A true Elizabethan.

ALASKAN MOOSE

Alaskan trains run slow.

Alaskan moose run loose.

However, even so,

The trains do goose the moose.

THE MOUNTAIN LION

The mountain lion

Fierce and fat

Is just another pussycat.

THE MUSKRAT

The muskrat despises his name.

For this he has no one to blame.

He is furry and fat,

Half musk and half rat,

Which drives this poor creature insane.

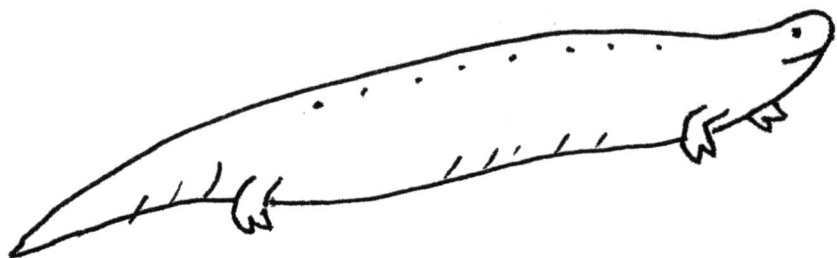

THE NEWT

The newt

Is cute.

However, it is never wise

For him to seek a beauty prize.

THE NIGHTINGALE

The melodious song of the nightingale

Is sung exclusively by the male.

That's why these males

Have such an abhorrence

Of people who call

Every nightingale "Florence."

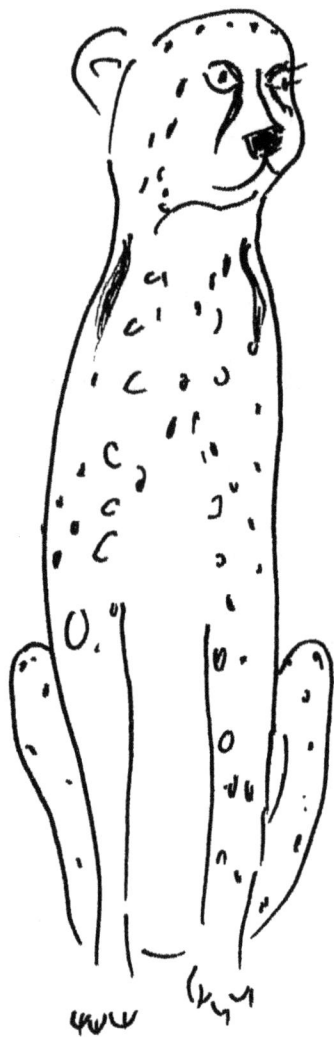

OCELOTS

When ocelots congregate together,

They never chat about the weather.

Instead, each ocelot complains

About his recent aches and pains;

The cost of medicines he buys,

And seeing spots before his eyes,

Sluggish livers, aching backs,

Our fauna hypochondriacs.

And that is why the ocelot

Appears to be so cross a lot.

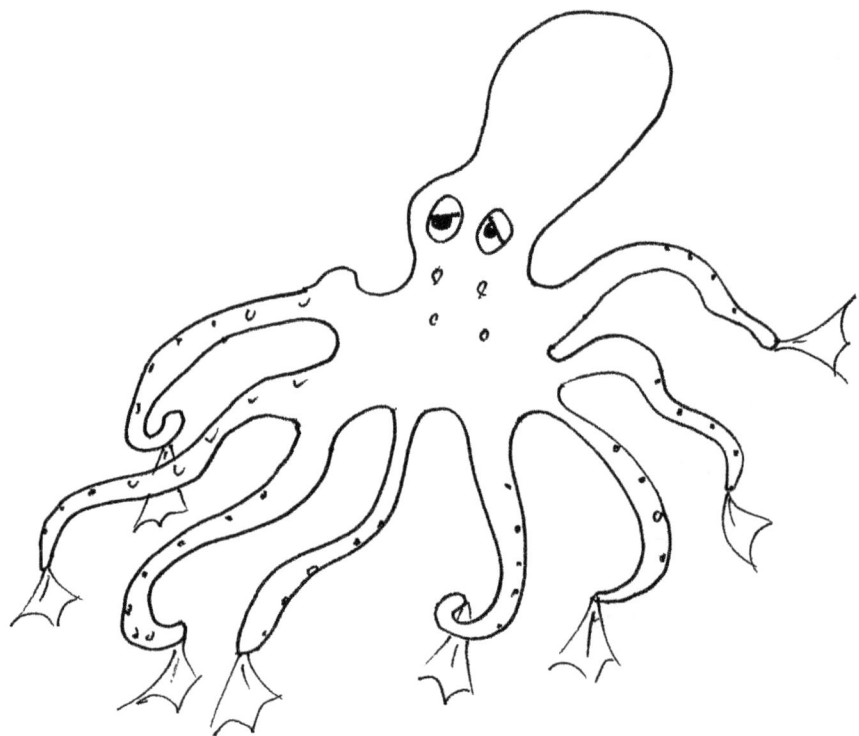

THE OCTOPUS

The sentimental octopus

With downcast, tearful eyes,

Pulls out eight pocket handkerchiefs

To wave his sad goodbyes.

AN OPOSSUM

An opossum —

Simply awesome.

A PARROT

A parrot often likes to say,

"Polly wants some crackers."

Other times she likes to say,

"I love the Green Bay Packers!"

THE PELICAN

The pelican perched upon his piling

Concentrates on simply smiling.

And though he does his level best

His beak sags down upon his chest.

The pelican should never try

To smile, but be content to fly,

Soaring about from place to place

With dignified and sober face.

A PERSIAN CAT

A fat Persian cat

Sits silently on a sill.

Does he leap to the ground

As soon as he's found

A venturesome mouse

Creeping into the house?

He won't

Or he might

Or he will.

PIGEONS

Pigeons prance and strut their stuff,

All puffy bust and dusty duff.

To them, they are the park coquettes.

To me, they'd make obnoxious pets.

PIGS IN SPAIN

The pampered pigs of Northern Spain

Take promenades in pouring rain.

Prim as poodles, peacock proud,

Each rosy snout is in a cloud.

The proper pigs of Southern Spain

Can also be considered vain.

Munching on acorns night and day,

While quoting Ernest Hemingway.

THE PTARMIGAN

The ptarmigan can change his coat

From summer brown to winter white.

He struts around for he is sure

He is a truly awesome sight.

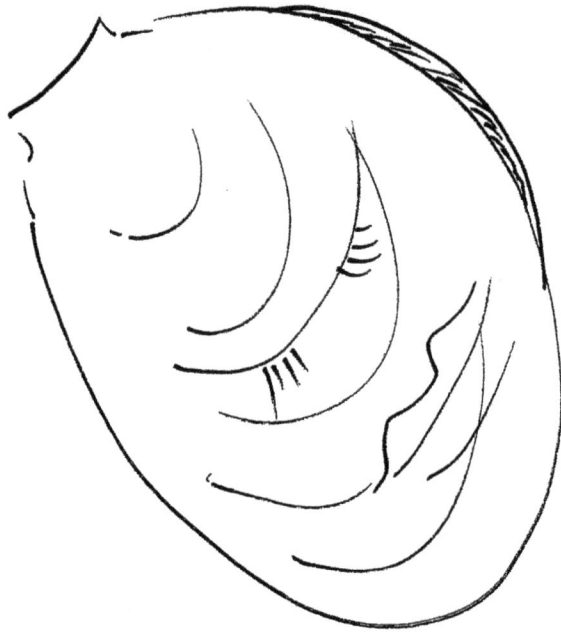

THE QUAHOG

Suggest that the quahog

Is not very glamorous,

And get from these clams

A cry that is clamorous.

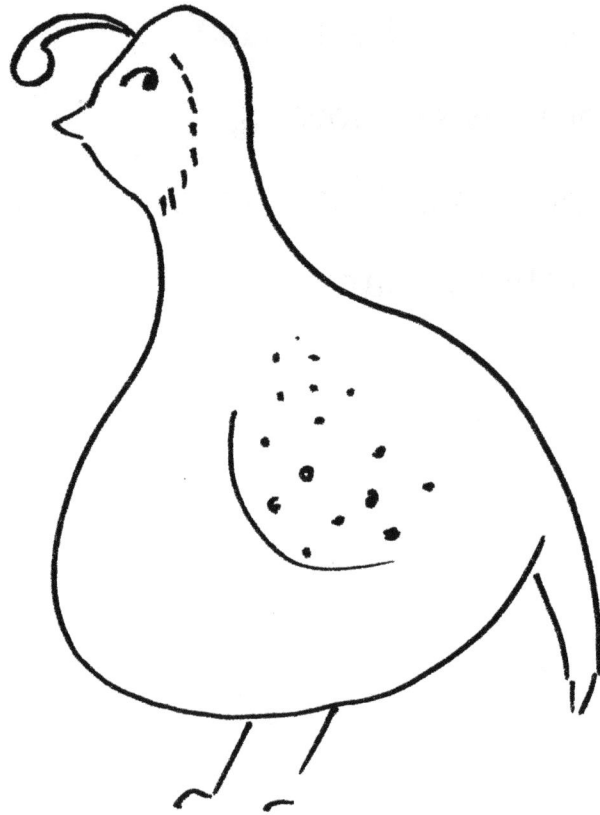

THE QUAIL

The quixotic quail

Has a very short tail,

Rather long, leggy legs,

And quite edible eggs.

The quail would like to be a knight,

And be addressed as Sir Bob White.

RABBITS

Rabbits have romantic habits

In and out of bed.

They seldom wait,

But simply mate,

And think of themselves as wed.

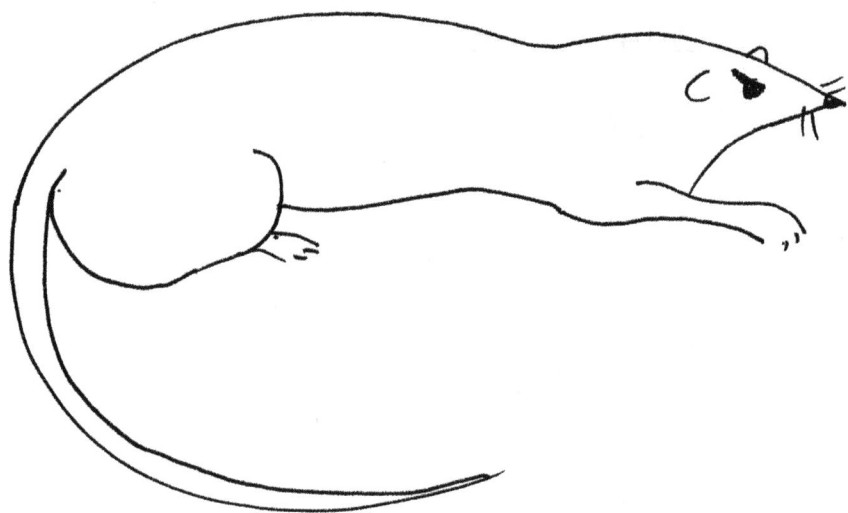

THE RAT

The remarkable rat

Is never too fat,

Though he always indulges in dinner,

Eating hot ratatouille,

Foods fatty and chewy.

He comes away sleeker and thinner!

REINDEERS

Here's something I can't explain:

Why reindeers are called "rein."

In fact, I know of no deer

Better called a snowdeer.

THE SATYR

The satyr is both goat and man,

A hearty party-loving Pan.

Some think of him as quite nefarious;

Others consider him just gregarious.

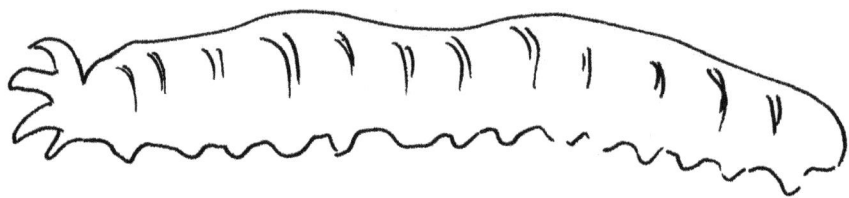

SEA CUCUMBERS

Sea cucumbers congregate in a group,

Floating around like somnolent lumps

Of vegetables in bowls of soup,

Tentacled heads and rounded rumps.

And when the tide deposits them

Under a coastal rock they spread,

To lie in holothurian clumps —

The ocean's sleepiest slugabed.

SHEEP

Sheep have woolly coats

Worn without a button.

Sheep when they are eaten

Are simply known as mutton.

SNAILS

Lazy snails

Leave oozy trails.

They're always slow —

The escargot.

THE TAPIR

Tapered tail and tapered toes,

Tapered body, tapered nose;

Easily cut from colored paper:

The tapered wild Malayan tapir.

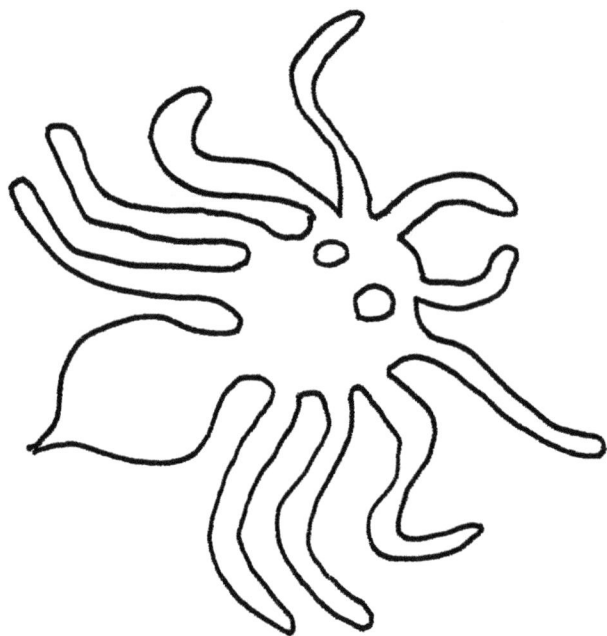

TARANTULAS

Tarantulas love to dance

Especially tarantellas.

It gives them a chance

To consider romance

Both the girl ones and the fellas.

THE TIGER

The tiger is ferocious when

His tail is tied in knots, for then

He shifts his stride to an angry swagger,

From cuddly cat to a testy tiger.

A TOAD

Ask a toad his favorite food,

A question he considers rude.

Why anyone would ask a toad,

We know he likes pie à la mode.

THE UNICORN

Behold the sad-faced unicorn,

Who was born with just one horn.

Another horn he ought to own:

A French horn or a saxophone.

THE URIAL

The urial is an Asian ram,

Who likes spring rolls with cherry jam.

They often help him get to sleep,

As well as simply counting sheep.

THE VOLE

The very voluptuous vole

Spends most of his time in a hole,

Where all he will want

Is a shrimp vole-au-vent

And some vichyssoise served in a bowl.

WATER BUFFALOS

Since water buffalos

Do not sweat,

They have to get

Their bodies wet.

So every day they follow

The path to a muddy hollow

And wallow.

A WOMBAT

If you sat on a wombat,

What would he say?

"I am neither a chair,

Nor a car, nor a sleigh.

So please, pretty please,

Will you please go away?"

A CURIOUS PET

X is an excellent pet.

I would like to describe it,

Or try to define it,

But nobody can but its vet.

THE YAK

The yak is from far-off Tibet.

With bad manners he's always upset.

He is rather loquacious,

Yet always most gracious,

He insists on correct etiquette.

THE ZEBRA

The zebra runs around

In stripes of black and white.

He likes this color scheme so much

He wears it day and night.

About the Author

A warning to him
Who would steal my purse:
All he will find
Is my witty light verse.

— Rosemary Butler

Rosemary Butler has enjoyed light verse for as long as she can remember. Throughout her extensive travels with her naval officer husband, from Europe to Asia, and from Alaska to the Philippines, she has written light verse on subjects that have caught her interest. She has especially enjoyed writing about animals—from testy tigers to remarkable rats. No animal can escape her pen!

In this book, Rosemary has used her pen not only to create animal verses, but also to illustrate them. In college at the University of Iowa, the University of Illinois, and Monmouth College, she studied art, art history, and set design. Photos of her art assemblages appear in *The Art of the Miniature*, by Jane Freeman; and two of her paintings were chosen to mark the opening of the National Library in Manila.

Rosemary has designed stage sets for college and community theaters. Her most memorable sets were for the Alaskan Armed Forces production of "South Pacific," which was performed at all major military bases in Alaska in 1951—the third company of this famous musical.

Besides being an artist, Rosemary has been a librarian, a researcher of Italian Renaissance paintings for the Lowe Art Museum at the University of Miami, and author of articles on Irish history, which were published in England and Ireland. In Ireland, Rosemary gave a lecture in the 13th-century round tower of Kilkenny Castle. Her subject was the life and times of Theobald Walter, the first Chief Butler of Ireland, a title created by King Henry II.

While living in Alaska, Rosemary wrote and produced a weekly children's program for the Armed Forces Radio Network. For the schools in Miami-Dade County, Florida, she wrote a slide program entitled "The Art of the Southwest Indians."

More recently, Rosemary wrote and illustrated a memoir about her travels in England, Ireland, and Spain. Her book, *Ghostly Encounters*, was published by Sun on Earth Books in 2010.

www.ingramcontent.com/pod-product-compliance
Lightning Source LLC
Chambersburg PA
CBHW050639150426

42813CB00054B/1122